WordPress for Beginners

Copyright © 2018

TABLE OF CONTENTS

Introduction...1

Step-By-Step Guide to Building a WordPress Website..............2

Install WordPress 4

Create your 1st Blog Post 13

Make Money Blogging 18

Introduction

It is very easy to start a WordPress website, and virtually anyone can do it. Choosing the wrong blogging platform is considered to be among the major mistakes committed by beginners when first initiating a blog. For around 95% of all users blogging, they choose to use WordPress.

Starting a blog is sure to be terrifying for every beginner, especially who are not computer savvy. It is very easy to start a WordPress Site, and virtually anyone can do it.

The website design can be customized with, different themes and plugins when installed. WordPress blog's visual appearance is theme controlled. Hence, as you visit your blog for the very first time, it will show something that will not be found interesting to many people. It becomes crucial on your part to change the theme to something interesting and exciting so that it can bring in that wow factor and be liked by everyone.

Step-By-Step Guide to Building a WordPress Website

There are over 15 million of websites running on the Content Management System (CMS). WordPress is the leader in CMS Platform that allows any newbie and expert to efficiently create and manage a website at a very affordable cost.

You get two options in WordPress:

➤ **Wordpress.com:** It is free but hosted by WordPress. It may be free but comes with certain limitations.

➤ **Wordpress.org**: You will be the owner of your website, but you have to buy your domain name and web host.

Let's go through the Step-by-Step process to create a WordPress website for beginners:

What is required to start?

➤ Three things will be essential to initiate WP blog:

➤ Domain name idea (it will be your blog's name, like wpbeginner.com)

➢ Web hosting account (where your site goes live on the web)

➢ For thirty minutes, your undivided attention

Step 1: Setup

➢ Domain name is what visitor's type in the web browser to find your site. It is the site's address on the web.

➢ Think of a good domain name for your business. If you decide to go with wordpress.com, you can get your domain name for free, but your domain will look like "mydomainname.wordpress.com". It is recommended to keep your domain name and hosting service separate from each other to maintain ownership of your domain.

➢ Web hosting is where the site goes live. Rather, it is the residence of your site on the web. Every website does require web hosting.

You can try out Bluehost, which is regarded to be an official hosting partner of WordPress. It offers free domain name and approximately 60% off with web hosting. You are free to choose your preferred domain + hosting at Webhostingsitereviews.com. Once completed, you get to log in to your cPanel or web hosting control panel from where you will be able to manage everything, ranging from emails, support, etc. It is here you install WordPress.

Install WordPress

You will come across small icons in dozens in the cPanel area for different features and services. It can be somewhat overwhelming for beginners. You can simply overlook 95% of them, as you will not need them immediately or at any point of time in the future. Scroll downwards to the site section. Click on WP icon. You will then get redirected to Quick Install section for WP. Click 'Get Started' button. The next screen will prompt you to choose your domain name. This you can select from the drop-down. Click Next. Once done, enter your website name, username as well as a password for your website. Also, you will be required to check all checkboxes, to proceed with your installation process. WP will start installing with Quick Install. You will be provided with options to browse through WP themes during the installation process. This is not necessary at this point in time and can be ignored. Once the installation is completed, you can view success notice appearing in the top header bar. Now, click Installation Complete link to be taken to the screen along with WP login password and URL.

Meet WordPress

WordPress is open source software you can use to create a
beautiful website, blog, or app.

Fill the form in Step 1 and then add your desired domain name
by clicking next.

Let's create a site

Please answer these questions so we can help you make the site you need.

What would you like to name your site?

> e.g. Mel's Diner, Stevie's Blog, Vail Renovations

What will your site be about?

> e.g. Fashion, travel, design, plumber, electrician

What's the primary goal you have for your site?

☐ Share ideas, experiences, updates, reviews, stories, videos, or photos

☐ Promote your business, skills, organization, or events

☐ Offer education, training, or mentoring

☐ Sell products or collect payments

☐ Showcase your portfolio

How comfortable are you with creating a website?

Beginner	1	2	3	4	5	Expert

Continue

If you have already purchased your preferred domain, then choose the "Already have a domain" option.

2. Singing up

Choosing a free web hosting service is fine, but a paid host ensures quality and control. At WordPress, you can find many hosts offers at an affordable rate.

3. Link your web host services with your domain name

When you sign up for hosting services, you will get the login information. Apart from that, you will also receive the nameservers from your host. The nameservers include two series of numbers. Copy those nameservers as you will need them in future. Now open your domain registrar and paste the copied nameserver in your domain name.

4. Install WordPress

Now you don't have to visit the WordPress page to install your WordPress script. Some hosts provide WordPress script in their script library for your convenience. First, log into your host account and search for WordPress script. When you find it, click on the install button, and you are all set for WordPress.

Before installing, you will be asked to provide your specific credentials such as admin name, new blog name, and email address. The information provided by you will be included in WordPress. If you want, you can rename your blog and change your email address anytime you want. After the installation of WordPress has been completed, you will get a link and password to your new WordPress site. You can change the password later.

You have successfully created your WP site! Your WP login URL is likely to appear in this manner:

http://yoursite.com/wp-admin

Now, click on WP login link for logging on to your dashboard. It is time to customize the overall appearance of your site and to start blogging.

5. Browsing the Dashboard of WordPress

Log into your WordPress website with your admin name and password. Then go to the dashboard. You will find a series of the menu on the left side of the dashboard.

The homepage of the Dashboard

Your Blog Posts: All your written blogs and posts will be displayed here.

> **Media**: All your media such as pictures, videos, etc. will be stored here. While writing a blog, you can directly add images and videos in this folder.

> **Pages**: All your static content will be stored here. You can save "About me" or "About Us" contents in this zone.

- ➤ **Comments**: Whatever comments you receive from your visitors will be stored here. You can manage the comments in this folder.

- ➤ **Appearance**: With this option, you can manage and customize the theme of your website. Organize, edit, and create menus for your theme here.

- ➤ **Plugins**: You can modify your plugins, add new plugins, delete old plugins, or update existing plugins.

- ➤ **Users**: You can add new users and allow them to modify your website on your behalf. The role which a user can play depends upon the permissions that you have granted.

- ➤ **Tools**: You can access your plugin settings through this menu. Also, you can import and export your WordPress data through tools.

- ➤ **Settings**: Set up your overall blog look through this menu.

Choose the theme for your WordPress

When you enter your WordPress website for the first time, you will get the default WordPress theme. To change your theme according to your choice, you can access the Theme library and change your WordPress theme. If you just want to modify your default theme, then choose the "Customize" option. If you want to change your theme, then click on New Theme and click the Activate button. If you want to select a theme from a different source, then add the downloaded theme to your WordPress Dashboard. Go to the "Add Themes" option and click on the "Upload Theme" button. After selecting your downloaded theme, click upload. Click on the Install button and then activate your new theme.

More on: Choose preferred WP Theme

Your WP blog's visual appearance is theme controlled. Hence, as your visit your blog for the very first time, it might be appearing something that will not be found interesting to many people. It becomes crucial on your part to change the theme to something interesting and exciting so that it can bring in that wow factor and be liked by everyone.

Customize the feel and look of your blog. This can be exciting and rewarding at the same time helping your site to transform into something beautiful and trendy. You can come across readymade WP themes in thousands which can be chosen and installed on your site. Few are paid, while others are available for free.

Changing your existing theme to a customized one is easy and effortless. You need to visit your WP dashboard and click on Appearance > Themes. Then click 'Add New Buttons.'

The next screen will help you to search WP themes amounting to around 4100, all of them available for free! You can find them at the Themes directory page of official WordPress.org. You can sort the themes by featured, latest, popular and by other feature filters (like layout, industry, etc.).

Once you have identified the theme that you wish to have on your site, place your mouse on it to display the Install button. Now click on the same and wait until the theme gets completely installed. Once done, an Activate button will replace the install button. Clicking the Activate button will help to activate the theme on your site. Once your theme has been installed successfully, you can now customize it according to your moods and preferences. Simply click on Customize link present under Appearance Menu.

As soon you have chosen your WP theme, now you are ready to initiate your very first blog post!

Create your 1ˢᵗ Blog Post

Your dreams of publishing posts in your own words and have followers in huge numbers is all set to be realized very soon. To start writing your very first blog post, simply click on Posts > Add New menu that is present on your WP dashboard! An editor area will appear where you can start writing your first blog post. After completing your writing, you should now click on Publish button present on the right side. Clicking it will publish your 1ˢᵗ blog post for the entire world to see and comment.

You will notice other sections present on posts screen, like Tags and Categories. These can be used to help organize all your blog posts. You are recommended to go through the difference between tags and categories and understand them clearly before you start writing the blog post. To use all features available on the post screen, you can get some assistance from WP help or from Google.

Beginners are often found to get confused between pages and posts menu present on WP's dashboard. It is for this reason, going through the difference between pages and posts in WP will be beneficial.

Setting up your sidebar widgets

Go to the "Appearance" menu and click on "Widgets." By default, you will see widgets such as "Recent Posts" and "Archives." Adding or removing a widget in WordPress in easy; you can even do this by drag and drop. You will find many widgets in WordPress serving different purposes. For Example, a text widget will allow you to add texts and code to your web pages.

Setting up plugins in WordPress

WordPress comes with millions of plugins that enhance the functions and user experience of your website. Some plugins that you should include in WordPress should be related to security, cache, SEO, and backup. Your focus should create a website that would run smoothly while offering safety from hackers. Just like you add the theme from the WordPress Library, you can add your plugins from the **Plugin** menu. You can also add plugins from other sources and add them to your plugin folder.

Click the **Install Now** button next to the plugin name, and it will be installed.

Customizations & Plugins

Once you have completed writing your first blog post, you should start including other usual features on your site like About Page, Contact Form, etc. To customize further as well as to add several other features like such as sliders, galleries, contact forms, etc. you will require making use of WP plugins. The latter are apps which allow the users to include new features to their website. Currently, there are 46,000+ WP plugins readily available for all users. The very best WP plugins are featured at WP Beginner to help new users to add the type of functionality that is desired and required. You can go through the step by step instruction to install WP plugin. Many beginners would like to know the type of plugins that are normally used on the website. To get such answers, it will be useful to check other's WP sites to find out the type of tools and plugins used by them. This does give a fair idea of what is to be used effectively to have an attractive and functional WP site.

Adding Content to WordPress

The first step you should perform is by adding static pages in your website. Your static pages should include your information, your company's information, Contact, Address, and anything related to that. Go to "Settings," click "Reading," then go to "Static Page" and select your desired posts or pages as your homepage. If you are a blogger, then leave the setting to default.

Make Money Blogging

You are now ready to start your blogging process, as you have completed all the process involving creating your blog and to customize it according to your particular preference and likes. You may be probably thinking, "How can I start making money from the blogging like others and become an expert". There are several ways by which you can monetize your blog successfully. However, you will not find any quick get rich scheme. Any such found are mere scams that you need to avoid and evade.

Here are a few ways to monetize your blog with Advertisements:

- ➤ GoogleAdSense.com
- ➤ Media.net
- ➤ Taboola.com
- ➤ Outbrain.com
- ➤ Clickbank.com

But to enjoy your efforts and to derive the rewards, you are expected to put in great efforts and hard work. You need to understand that there is no such shortcut to achieve success in life.

Step 7: Master WordPress

It is essential on your part to expand your existing WP knowledge, to enhance your site, ensure everyone likes it and to monetize it. You will want to get familiar with the following:

> ➢ WPBeginner Blog: It is the central place to derive all WP tutorials.
> ➢ WPBeginner Videos: If you are new to WordPress, then watching the videos can help you to master WP.
> ➢ WPBeginner Dictionary: It is indeed the best place to be for beginners to familiarize themselves with WP lingo and start blogging.

You should also subscribe to WP's YouTube Channel to enjoy watching informative video tutorials to learn WP and become more effective and to achieve immense success.

Promoting your Website

The last step includes the promotion of your website. Create your contents according to your target audience. To market your site, choose SEO and SMO methods.

Setting up a blog on your website should be a simple and exciting process if you choose to use the above website builders. Make sure you provide informative, engaging and exciting content on your blog for the best outcome. Settingupablog.org has a **free guide** to going around setting up a blog with ease.

I am glad I have been able to teach you tips and avenues. I would love to hear feedback if you found this book valuable. ***Please leave a positive review if this book has positively impacted you.***

Until then, stay connected!

WordPress Alternatives

Weebly is an excellent free website builder that you should consider if you want to build your website with ease and faster. It's free and simple to use, which means you should select it when setting up a blog on your site.

Wix is a website builder that lets you create a free website that looks the way you want. For example, it provides you with professional image collections, personalized domains, secure hosting and beautiful galleries. Wix websites are automatically mobile optimized, which means that your site will look stunning to visitors.

www.ingramcontent.com/pod-product-compliance
Lightning Source LLC
Chambersburg PA
CBHW052143070326
40690CB00047B/2051